The Caterpillar and his Maker

Book One

JOSHUA OSIME

Exulon ELITE

Copyright © 2015 by Joshua Osime

The Caterpillar and his Maker
Book One
by Joshua Osime

Illustrated by Richie Williams

Printed in the United States of America.

Edited by Xulon Press

ISBN 9781498442299

All rights reserved solely by the author. The author guarantees all contents are original and do not infringe upon the legal rights of any other person or work. No part of this book may be reproduced in any form without the permission of the author. The views expressed in this book are not necessarily those of the publisher.

Unless otherwise indicated, Scripture quotations are taken from the King James Version (KJV) – public domain

Author owns all copyright in text and illustrations.

www.xulonpress.com

Dedication

This collection of thoughts in print is dedicated to my brother, **The Hon. Theophilus Azebe-Osime,** who went to be with the Lord on Sunday, January 13, 2002.

Thank God, his soul is resting in peace.

Amen.

Introduction

Several years ago, I was lazing around alone when, in my spirit, I heard, loudly and clearly, the words, "Men are like caterpillars".

Who? Me? A caterpillar? The air seemed to be suddenly still, under the shade of the mango tree that sheltered me from the tropical sun, as I reflected on this summation. The Spirit of my Father had, doubtlessly, answered this young mind's quest to understand life.

Wait, what does a green, hairy, chubby, multi-legged, negative IQ creature have in common with man? Man, the apex of creation; man, the articulate and intelligent one? Or, was he?

Pondering has its profits. In the weeks, months and years following, incremental clarity by the Spirit of God began to settle on me. The day came when I had to set these "revelations" to paper, and the piece "The Caterpillar and his Maker" was born.

Just as with a buffet spread, I soon encountered a myriad of items on life's menu to which my interest was directed. As soon as my mental taste buds partook of the sour, sweet, salty, bitter and even the repugnant, inspiration surged within me and several other poetic pieces were birthed. With the Word of God as my measure, I soon saw that I was setting forth God's truth in verse and stanza; I loved it.

God willing, we would publish other poetic pieces at their set times; these have been collated as a first volume. I pray they bless you.

Joshua

Table of Contents

Dedication v
Introduction vii

1. Compassion 11
2. Human Cargo 13
3. The Gangster 15
4. Bondage 17
5. That Race 20
6. Snow 22
7. The Caterpillar and his Maker 24
8. Hate 28
9. He was a good man… 31
10. Crossroads 34
11. My Father the Terrible 37
12. Hammered 39
13. Pledge 42
14. Make my day! 44
15. For The One That I Love 47
16. The Burden 49
17. The Setup 52
18. Who is fooling whom? 56

19. I pray for that Peace 58
20. Just Asking 60
21. Prayer 63
22. The Man 65
23. The Impressive Shell 67
24. The Unchanger................................ 69

Compassion

Where has your compassion gone?
You'd always like a favor, but to others you'd render none.
Do you think he likes the street corner?
To you, he is a drug-ravaged goner,
Or a good-for-nothing loser.
But have you ever looked a little closer?
It could be your son, your dad, holding that bowl;
Then, doubtless, he is a hardworking, but luckless soul.
Which goggles do you have on?
For your presumptions, you should mourn.
Surely, from you, he will find no help,
You lack money, food, and clothes; moreover, your lion just had her whelp!
Okay!
Pray life deals you no blow,
Because you'd be praying the traffic was slow,
And that someone in all that motion,
Will look at you and have some compassion.

1 John 3:17 But whoso hath this world's good, and seeth his brother have need, and shutteth up his bowels of compassion from him, how dwelleth the love of God in him?

Proverbs 21:13 Whoso stoppeth his ears at the cry of the poor, he also shall cry himself, but shall not be heard.

Proverbs 19:17 He that hath pity upon the poor lendeth unto the LORD; and that which he hath given will he pay him again.

Human Cargo

They are now getting quite old,
The ones that gave you entrance.
A zillion hours they spent,
Tending to your enormous needs.
Sleepless and restless they surged on: drugged,
Doped by the love for your tender and cute self.
Headaches, heartaches, backaches, and arm aches,
You fed them to the fill.
Aches for breakfast and aches for dinner;
In return for the love and care they fed you.
What an exchange!
But they never took you to court,
Pleading your unfair practices.
They accepted to be short-changed by you,
Hoping to see a mature human emerge from your pesky self.
Now you and your siblings are grown,
And these persons are burdens to your sophisticated lives.
Jointly, and severally, you all lack resources
To nurture these ones in their twilight years;
Or care for them personally or vicariously.
What next?
Call UPS and ship them away!
Ship them with no return address,
To a forsaken home to ebb away!
And on with your jolly lives!

Your siblings and you should wait but a little while,
For in a little while, you and they *will* get old.
Well, hopefully....

Deuteronomy 5:16 Honour thy father and thy mother, as the LORD thy God hath commanded thee; that thy days may be prolonged, and that it may go well with thee, in the land which the LORD thy God giveth thee.

The Gangster

So you think you are powerful?
Five of you pouncing on him can be quite a handful.
You all have clubs, knives, and guns;
Deadly weapons, even in the hands of nuns.
But what did he do?
He tampered with your ego a time or two.
Wouldn't join your gang, or let you be his boss:
Wouldn't waste his time on an ignoble cause.
So, his every word or deed causes you an irritation;
His argument with your girlfriend last night — an unpardonable infraction.
Now his armor-plated skin is cut, his steel bones broken:
Your cohorts acting on the commands you had spoken.
Five cowards lording over the helpless;
Evidently, you are all quite shameless.
Pray, if you think you have so much power,
Why not go one-on-one with a pugilist for an hour?

2 Chronicles 26:16a But when he was strong, his heart was lifted up to his destruction:

Job 40:7, 9 Gird up thy loins now like a man: I will demand of thee, and declare thou unto me. Hath thou an arm like God? or canst thou thunder with a voice like him?

Bondage

Mind intact;
Will un-coerced;
Limbs swing freely;
Wholly voluntarily —
Or so it seemed...
But the man was a puppet,
For his hands, legs, head were stringed.
Cords firmly attached where
The man had granted access,
Or where he had guarded without success.
So he logically did the irrational
And, with a sound mind, did the insane.

Yet his eyes,
Those sharp, piercing eyes,
Saw not strong strings strapped;
Stayed at several segments.
His keen ears
Heard not the clinking chains,
Connecting one limb to another:
Foot to foot,
Hand to hand.
His vices of choice,
Snares of flesh and soul;
Taking turns at the remote strings,
Pulling and plucking
Like a maestro on his guitar...

The man was bound.
Worse —
He knew it not.
The master knew not that he was the slave.
The warden knew not that he was the captive.
The man was at once in prison,
Yet walking free;
Like the snail
Carrying his jail,
He went,
Calling his cell his home —
His captors his pleasure;
His chains his amusement;
His degradation his enjoyment...

When will you perceive,
O deaf and blind one?
See and hear depletion around you —
On you —
Subtraction, division,
Erosion, corrosion:
Your soul ebbing away
Slowly...
When will you perceive?

Proverbs 5:22 His own iniquities shall take the wicked himself, and he shall be holden with the cords of his sins.

Proverbs 21:16 The man that wandereth out of the way of understanding shall remain in the congregation of the dead.

That Race

How did you get in that race?
You sure are moving at a fast pace!
You must have put in a lot of hard work;
You seem as hot as a bowl of molten rock.
When *you carefully* selected your team, you were in no trance;
A decision your *inferior competitors* had left to chance.
Now you seem to be ahead of the pack,
While they all seem to be staring at your back.
You don't understand what I'm talking about?
Why, then, do you want to engage me in a bout?
I was just asking how *you* got in *that* race;
I mean the one with the color of your face.
One would think your race *you* chose to join,
And for all others, *God* had to *flip* a coin.
Think; you will know it's not true.
Then question, why your superior pride you continually brew.

Acts 17:24a, 26 God that made the world and all things therein, ...hath made of one blood all nations of men for to dwell on all the face of the earth, and hath determined the times before appointed, and the bounds of their habitation;

Ephesians 2:14-15 For he is our peace, who hath made both one, and hath broken down the middle wall of partition between us; Having abolished in his flesh the enmity, even the law of commandments contained in ordinances; for to make in himself of twain one new man, so making peace;

Snow

"Yes, snow."
"What else do I need to show?"

Lord, how You freeze each flake they do not know,
Nor how You make their blood to flow.
How the seed they sow,
Into a tall tree will grow;
Yet Your name they want to mow;
'Tis like trying to make Kilimanjaro low,
Or putting Mount Everest in tow.
Lord, Your nostril You will blow,
And like burning coals, they will glow.
Unless their doubts they throw;
By You, away from their sins go,
And hurry to come kiss Your big toe.
Lord, snow is proof enough; You to show…

Psalms 19:1-3 The heavens declare the glory of God; and the firmament sheweth his handywork. Day unto day uttereth speech, and night unto night sheweth knowledge. There is no speech nor language, where their voice is not heard.

Romans 1:20 For the invisible things of him from the creation of the world are clearly seen, being understood by the things that are made, even his eternal power and Godhead; so that they are without excuse:

The Caterpillar and his Maker

One hot, sunny afternoon,
Long before the reawakening of the moon,
Caterpillar perched on a narrow grass blade.
He was hairy, green, and chubby, and looked like he had it made.
He looked around nervously for his nightmare:
A bird, a boy, a lawnmower weren't so rare.
He then started munching and stuffing his mouth to the fill,
Rejoicing at the expanse of chlorophyll.
Not that he could see very far,
But his myopic eyes could not his enthusiasm mar.

In comes Maker, for the umpteenth time,
Seeking to preserve caterpillar with His rhyme.
"Pause a little while, my dear,"
Maker's voice ever so gentle but clear;
"I made you for better things than this —
Not to crawl your way through life sans peace,
Or forever wriggle and chew on the tasteless.
On that schedule, life is worthless....
But your change can only come,
If you embrace all My words, not some.
In limbo, in your mother's egg, you were,
Before I made you a caterpillar and brought you here.
You must die to what you now know as you;
Entering a cocoon is what I'll have you do.
And from thence be reborn,
A breathless spectacle you'll become.
Yea, but all these can only come to pass
If My Word you let not slip by like gas."

Good ol' green and chubby caterpillar,
Looked around again for a killer,
And then passed on his Maker's words to his brain;
A *huge* organ, albeit no bigger than a grain.
At the widest part, one-sixteenth of an inch across;
If you sought to find it, you'd certainly be at a loss.
"Are my Maker's words rational or true?" he queried;
To stop the daily wriggle and chewing seemed so horrid.
"Is there anything else to do,
Than to dangle on a leaf or two;
Eat on to your heart's content
Hang out with your buddies and never relent?"

Caterpillar's gigantic brain then replied,
"I've done all possible analyses: your Maker lied."
Caterpillar, disbelieving, choose his Maker to doubt:
His mind, his brain, never fathoming that from which he just missed out.
Multicolored wings to sail through the air,
Could a butterfly look so fair?
A change of diet, the sweet for the tasteless;
A change of lifestyle, the airborne for the flightless;
A connoisseur of flower wines,
My, my, my, God has soooooo many vines.

But it wasn't so long thereafter,
When Caterpillar, as usual, had skipped his siesta,
Surfeiting to his heart's content —
He really seemed to be hell-bent —
That he heard a rumble,
'Twas a lawnmower chomping grass on the double.
Caterpillar sought to flee,
His wonder brain no more full of glee.
"Maker! Master!" he called,
"Save me from this monster machine!" he bawled.
The words had no sooner left his lips,
When Caterpillar was silenced for keeps.
The mower had rolled swiftly by:
Leaf, flower, and all in its path had to die.

Let us now peek in the mirror,
And hopefully *the caterpillar* looking might see the one in error.
Where are we really heading?
Peace and life, or that which is death yielding?
What choices are we making?
Our lives are ours for the baking.
One question needs be answered before we dine:
"Am I using my Maker's recipe or mine?"

Proverbs 14:12 There is a way which seemeth right unto a man, but the end thereof are the ways of death.

Proverbs 3:5-6 Trust in the LORD with all thine heart; and lean not unto thine own understanding. In all thy ways acknowledge Him, and He shall direct thy path.

John 3:3 Jesus answered and said unto him, "Verily, verily, I say unto thee, Except a man be born again, he cannot see the kingdom of God."

1 Corinthians 2:14 But the natural man receiveth not the things of the Spirit of God: for they are foolishness unto him: neither can he know them, because they are spiritually discerned.

Hate

Hate:
That potent fuel,
On which many run.
A war propellant;
Renewable,
Inexhaustible, for those who have so chosen.
No centrifuges,
No noxious emissions,
Only evil thoughts and machinations;
Albeit more toxic than their tangible relatives.
Cankerous,
Consuming the hater more than the hated;
Worse than a Chernobyl within,
At once, empowering and destructive.
Like a match blazing in explosive power,
Only for its head, nay, its totality,
To translate into a lump of ash in the aftermath...

In the aftermath of hate,
Mission accomplished:
Hated harpooned, as hater had hatched it.
Hate abated.
Hater's numbness lifts;
The floods of pain come gushing in.
System check:
Lethal levels of venomous hate-waste
Saturate the hater's being.
Slow death.
Long misery.
Anginas of guilt.
Migraines of regret.

Hate:
Some cheap and deadly fuel.
Hater,
Why not try love instead...

Romans 13:10a Love worketh no ill to his neighbour....

1 John 4:10 Herein is love, not that we loved God, but that he loved us, and sent his Son to be the propitiation for our sins.

1 John 4:8 He that loveth not knoweth not God; for God is love.

He was a good man…

"He was a good man…"

Oh, shut up!
If you have nothing to say,
Say nothing.
He lies stiff in his casket,
And you have all gathered:
Sham eulogizers and pretenders
Liars —
That's more like it.
You still wish you could strangle his lifeless body;
That unrepentant, vain, lying, stealing, profane,
*Adulterous, back-stabbing **"friend"** of yours,*
That cared for you as a hawk would care for a chicken.

But listen to you:
"He was such a wonderful friend,
A godly husband and father.
He had such a good heart,
And put everyone else before himself.
Never a harsh word; always a word to edify.
An excellent example of a Christian.
You could trust him with your life;
And now, he is looking down on us from heaven…"

Stop! Stop!! Stooooop!!!
Even the priest is bent over, nauseated;
Puking at the profuseness of your phony profession.
Your conning of the congregation.

I presume not to frame words for you, sir,
But if there is nothing to be said,
*Let nothing **be** said.*
But add a prayer for his family,
And all others his crooked life affected,
Forcing facial flashfloods.
Do keep his service brief,
And give everyone relief;
Because new lies
Attract new flies,
That will buzz around your already agitated soul.

Proverbs 14:32 The wicked is driven away in his wickedness: but the righteous hath hope in his death.

Job 32:21-22 Let me not, I pray you, accept any man's person, neither let me give flattering titles unto man. For I know not to give flattering titles; in so doing my maker would soon take me away.

Isaiah 57:21 There is no peace, saith my God, to the wicked.

Crossroads

Crossroads:
The place of decision;
The place where the shadow of your doubts
Seeks to have a life of its own;
Where the voice of your fears
Seems to boast of more decibels;
Where the troops of indecision
Compass the fortress of your mind,
Stalking it like a prized prey;
Sending forth sniper fire —
Sleek, sharp shots — thoughts —
Through the crevices of your mind.
Sent to weaken your resolve, your faith,
Battering rams —
Your seemingly intractable circumstances,
Buffeting you on all sides.

Crossroads:
The place where it seems to be required
That you hurdle Everest,
Or swim the Pacific.
The place of endless torment,
Gallons of mind fuel burnt:

Needlessly,
Endlessly,
Entropy.
That place not to tarry long at,
Lest you be wearied by strife;
Internal combustion,
Slow exhaustion.

Before you call those you know, call Him who knows you;
Receive His instructions and act.
Act quick and cast down the strongholds of the mind —
Those pockets of insurrection,
Erupting within your fortress.
Let your mind flow as one river not twain,
Then surely will a highway appear
Spanning the ocean,
Built by stones quarried:
Yes, from that level field that once housed your Everest.

James 1:5-8 If any of you lack wisdom, let him ask of God, that giveth to all men liberally, and upbraideth not; and it shall be given him. But let him ask in faith, nothing wavering. For he that wavereth is like a wave of the sea driven with the wind and tossed. For let not that man think that he shall receive anything of the Lord. A double mind man is unstable in all his ways.

John 2:5 His mother saith unto the servants, Whatsoever he saith unto you, do it.

Isaiah 43:19 Behold, I will do a new thing; now it shall spring forth; shall ye not know it? I will even make a way in the wilderness, and rivers in the desert.

Mark 10:27 And Jesus looking upon them saith, "With men it is impossible, but not with God: for with God all things are possible."

My Father the Terrible

My Father is terrible,
That's Old English to say He is incredible.
To Him, impossibilities are edible.
Wide Red Seas passable.
The hard and dry yield the drinkable.
To parley with the sinner is not unthinkable.
The lowest of the lost redeemable;
To my Father, these are the most loveable,
For their sins are no more knowable.
Lost in depths to the accuser unreachable.
The measure of His love is incalculable.
His wisdom is unsearchable.
An encounter with Him unforgettable;
That's my Father the Terrible.

Psalm 66:1-3 Make a joyful noise unto God, all ye lands: Sing forth the honour of his name: make his praise glorious. Say unto God, How terrible art thou in thy works! through the greatness of thy power shall thine enemies submit themselves unto thee.

Romans 5:8 But God commendeth his love toward us, in that, while we were yet sinners, Christ died for us.

Mark 2:16 And when the scribes and Pharisees saw him eat with publicans and sinners, they said unto his disciples, How is it that he eateth and drinketh with publicans and sinners?

Hammered

It was amusing at first;
Jones the Reticent had become more ebullient.
His tongue loosened a notch or so:
A syllable or two had replaced his oath of silence.
He responded when you said hi
And he smiled a little now.
It was a welcome change from his stoic screensaver,
His face engravement.
A little conversation had replaced the glare...

Then it became intriguing.
In the span of a few hours,
A human being was morphing before me.
From one end of the spectrum
Towards the frontiers of the other, he went.
The Stoic One had now become loquacious.
The cool koala was starting to buzz like a bee.
Jones was defrosting, fast —
Like a freezer open and unplugged....

It then became saddening, alarming.
This grown man:
Respectable, strong,
Honorable —
Well, at least a few hours ago —
Was now a sad spectacle.
The grave, measured steps of the tortoise

Had evolved,
Right before my eyes,
To the rapid steps of a hare —
With eight legs —
Each leg having a mind of its own,
Like a millipede with dementia…..

So went Jones,
Walking tall like a tower
Of the not-so-vertical kind,
This tower, oscillating between perpendicularity
And acrobat-like body inclines,
Like a palm tree tossed to and fro by a hurricane –
Make that several hurricanes —
The genie hurricanes that Jones summoned from each bottle he emptied.
Now the strong winds swirl within,
Even though it is blue skies without….
Jones was getting hammered…

Ahhh……
But he will be here tomorrow,
Imbibing to the overflow,
Some more liquid hurricanes.
I already can see the hammer falling…….

Proverbs 20:1 Wine is a mocker, strong drink is raging: and whosoever is deceived thereby is not wise.

Isaiah 5:11, 22 Woe unto them that rise up early in the morning, that they may follow strong drink; that continue until night, till wine inflame them! Woe unto them that are mighty to drink wine, and men of strength to mingle strong drink:

Proverbs 23:19-21 Hear thou, my son, and be wise, and guide thine heart in the way. Be not among winebibbers; among riotous eaters of flesh: For the drunkard and the glutton shall come to poverty: and drowsiness shall clothe a man with rags.

Pledge

To the One that called me,
I pledge to be faithful,
Not hateful.
Your love will I declare:
Your saints prepare.
A tool I am for your harvest:
For in me, You daily invest
Your will, Your word.
In my hands, You've placed Your sword
To plunder darkness
And to the lost be a witness.
With power, with proof,
I see some tearing up a roof …
Oh, dear Lord,
Help me be faithful…

Proverbs 20:6 Most men will proclaim every one his own goodness: but a faithful man who can find?

Ezekiel 34:2 Son of man, prophesy against the shepherds of Israel, prophesy, and say unto them, Thus saith the Lord GOD unto the shepherds; Woe be to the shepherds of Israel that do feed themselves! should not the shepherds feed the flocks?

Jeremiah 12:10 Many pastors have destroyed my vineyard, they have trodden my portion under foot, they have made my pleasant portion a desolate wilderness.

Philippians 4:13 I can do all things through Christ which strengtheneth me.

Make my day!

Good God Almighty, what can I say?
Bitter, Sweet, Hot or Cold: You always make my day.
Your hand lifting up the fallen,
Or souls liberated by Your calling,
Is always a wonder, a sight to see;
You fill them with peace, and still no fee!
A baby born — Your creation he'll behold.
Rain, Sun, Harvest – all Your mercies can't be told.

Good God Almighty, what can I say?
In Your name, all my enemies are kept at bay.
They come with chains and shackles, hooks and tackles.
At Thy word, they flee faster than a pack of jackals.
You've stomped my fears and made me walk in dominion,
And daily fellowship with You in holy communion.
When the enemy comes and tries to have me bound,
I let him know my Lord beat him in the first round.

Good God Almighty, what can I say?
Deserts, rivers, whatever: You always make a way.
For Your beloved, You will rebuke the sea
And rain down the meals he can't see.
To see the smiles on the healed and the freed
Is my hunger, my greed.
Make me an instrument, a witness of Your way.
Good God Almighty, please make my day!

Good God Almighty, the One that makes a way:
Saving, Healing, Cleansing, Giving, every single day.
To be Your eyes, Your ears,
Your lips, Your hands to wipe away the tears;
To see You bless;
To help my brethren to Thy prize to press;
To see You make a way
Is how You make my day.

Luke 4:18-19 The Spirit of the Lord is upon me, because he hath anointed me to preach the gospel to the poor; he hath sent me to heal the brokenhearted, to preach deliverance to the captives, and recovering of sight to the blind, to set at liberty them that are bruised, To preach the acceptable year of the Lord.

For The One That I Love

The One who loved me
Has been, and is, kind and gracious.
He knew that alone I wouldn't want to be,
So He sent one so sweet and delicious.
From the vaults of my heart,
My Lord pulled my dreams and thoughts,
And beckoned that I see what with them He had wrought.
What I saw made me shout,
"Wow! Look what I got!!"
She is better than what my heart had yearned for:
More precious than what my hands could dig for;
Rarer than my eyes could seek for;
Yet meek and sweet.
This proud world cannot with her compete.
She is the one that I love,
Sent by the One who loved me....

Song 1:15 Behold, thou art fair, my love; behold, thou art fair; thou hast doves' eyes.

Proverbs 18:22 Whoso findeth a wife findeth a good thing, and obtaineth favour of the LORD.

Proverbs 19:14b ...and a prudent wife is from the LORD.

The Burden

The load of sin is heavy,
It holds back pain in your soul, like a levee.
Denial won't ease the strain on your marrow,
'Tis like running from your shadow.
What would alleviate this inner grief?
Oh, my good Lord, grant me relief.
Thy Commandment I had broken:
This lump of clay going against that You had spoken.
My good Lord, have mercy,
My sin is all I see.
'Tis like a bad dream in instant replay,
Daytime, nighttime: it seeks my soul to slay.

Lord,
Do you still draw me near?
My body trembles from Thy fear.
Lord,
Would you not depart from this man and his sin?
Oh, how I long to be clean!!!
In Thy precious blood, Lord, dip me.
Loosen me from this guilt that has gripped me.
That with a clear conscience, I may serve Thee.
In this state of filth, don't let me be.

From vanity, my Lord, my eyes prevent:
My hands restrain that they do not evil invent.
An evil word may my lips not utter:
Help me lift the fallen from the gutter.
Let my heart grieve for what grieves You.
Let my will yield to what You'd have me do.
Oh my Lord, guard my heart.
Let it be clean each and every part,
So that this lump of clay
May in Your presence lay:
Purified,
Undefiled,
Free from the torments of the sin warden.
For I no more carry his burden...

Isaiah 1:18 "Come now, and let us reason together," saith the LORD: "though your sins be as scarlet, they shall be as white as snow; though they be red like crimson, they shall be as wool."

John 8:36 If the Son therefore shall make you free, ye shall be free indeed.

Matthew 11:28 Come unto me, all ye that labour and are heavy laden, and I will give you rest.

The Setup

We took off from yonder,
The place of Glory and Wonder:
Destination Earth.
To our several ports we had to berth:
Some afar off, some right down the street;
Some in languages in which I couldn't greet.
In we came via motherhood.
Siblinghood became lost in nationhood.
To each a separate time, place, inventory.
As I grew older, I started reading my history.

Inventory check complete.
All my parts were replete:
Two hands, two legs, two eyes all the same.
Alas, my sibling down the street — he was lame.
I could walk, talk, and climb a tree:
Co-sojourner had eyes that could not see.
Clothes on my back, roof o'er my head, my hands on a meal:
Brother's stomach yearned for a hot morsel to feel.
I guess good grades meant I was smart,
But my buddy in class had to drop out...

The more I read my history, the more I grew curious.
Some had been less fortunate and that some wasn't us.
I saw them everywhere,
The object of all that could stare:
Homeless, clothesless,
Limbless, sightless;
Some in pain, some insane.
Reclaiming self-dignity was gain.
Then the question in me arose:
Why was I nestled in a rose?

Why I not them, my Lord?
Why them, not I, with some missing mud?
Why look I forward to my meals,
And they to the peels?
Laid up in the waste dump,
Where some would not even let their dogs jump.
Not for my deeds or thoughts surely,
My sins will overflow a lorry.
Oh my good Lord, why?
It's tough to understand, need I try?

Then came His Word,
Which in me did strike a chord.
"***You saw me*** hungry and didn't feed me,
Thirsty, and a drink you wouldn't give me,
Sick, but you wouldn't visit me,
Naked and your extra shirt couldn't find me."
These words were to ***us,*** not ***them:***
These words were to ***us,*** not ***them:***
Again, these words were to ***us,*** not ***them:***
Us, all, that had something that to another was a gem.
Legs, hands, eyes — all from Him that us did bless.
A smile, good health, strength — the list is endless.

He will not come to us in a train of glamour,
But my Lord daily will us clamor.
For Agape, for love;
For others needs to solve.
Not to play the blame game,
But to put love in action and not just call His name.
To abide with Him on high is our goal.
But how many will stoop to his neighbor who is low?

Our prayers we always want Him to answer.
Others' prayers to us — we send to the bouncers.

What is this earth, this life for?
Why has it been in existence since the days of yore?
It's a nursery, a breeding ground.
It's for our enjoyment, yet a proving ground;
A gateway to the eternal.
Our own deeds we'll see, so we can't be in denial
On that Great Day of Judgment.
Too late it will be **then** to make an amendment.
For the Lord surely will us weed
And remove those that yielded no fruit from His Seed.
With lack of love and evil, He will not put up.
Yeah, this life was a setup...

1 Peter 4:10 As every man hath received **the gift**, even so minister **the same** one to another, as good stewards of the manifold grace of God.

Job 31:15 Did not he that made me in the womb make him? and did not one fashion us in the womb?

Matthew 25:44-45 Then shall they also answer him, saying, Lord, when saw we thee an hungred, or athirst, or a stranger, or naked, or sick, or in prison, and did not minister unto thee? Then shall he answer them, saying, Verily I say unto you, Inasmuch as ye did it not to one of the least of these, ye did it not to me.

Who is fooling whom?

Slick, smooth and sanctified:
Hallelujahs by day,
Unmentionables by night.
Superclean in full view,
Extra filthy in no view.
Who is fooling whom?

High decibel wailings,
Cool gyrations:
Stoopings, swoonings
Groanings, moanings
From the aquifer of the Spirit.
Wading in the deep waters of the Almighty...

Or is it all Broadway,
Perhaps Hollywood –
A ***Pseudo Pneuma Production:***
Every word, move, gesture mastered,
Delivered flawlessly.
High drama in the House of God,
But who is fooling whom?

The One we have to deal with
Looks not with the eyes of men.
We can hide our hearts and hands from Him,
If fish can hide from water.
Your fellow fish you might deceive,
But the Water from which your life you receive,
Will perceive,
All that you ever do or conceive.

Pray,
Who is fooling whom?

Proverbs 15:3 The eyes of the LORD are in every place, beholding the evil and the good.

Job 27: 8 For what is the hope of the hypocrite, though he hath gained, when God taketh away his soul?

Isaiah 33:14-17 The sinners in Zion are afraid; fearfulness hath surprised the hypocrites. Who among us shall dwell with the devouring fire? who among us shall dwell with everlasting burnings? He that walketh righteously, and speaketh uprightly; he that despiseth the gain of oppressions, that shaketh his hands from holding of bribes, that stoppeth his ears from hearing of blood, and shutteth his eyes from seeing evil;

I pray for that Peace

I pray for that Peace....
The one where the offsprings of Noah
Would realize their brotherhood:
Where tyrants and despots lay in ICUs,
Recovering from heart transplants.
The warm and fleshy,
Pumping in place of the cold and stony.
The Peace where
Two .38s lurk no more in those baggy pants,
But the pockets swell
With blessings for his neighbor.
I pray for the continuous laughter of children playing:
That priceless, indescribably sweet music to the ears.
The Peace where the enmity of God's creatures would vaporize:
Cub and Kid, Boy and Bear playing,
Uttering sounds of joy.
I pray for that Peace....

Isaiah 11:7 And the cow and the bear shall feed; their young ones shall lie down together: and the lion shall eat straw like the ox.

Just Asking

With utmost respect, my friend,
Do I venture to ask these questions...

Just looking at your family tree,
I am awestruck by your formidable ancestry...
So your great-grandfather was an ape?
Your great-Uncle Willy a slick tuna?
Matriarch Matilda an alligator,
And cousin Patrick a frog?
Who are those vultures?
Oh, my apologies, I had drifted into your in-laws tree...

Ahem, where were we?
Yes... I wish your family tree could all be brought back to life,
'Cause your family reunion would be quite a sight:
Lots of croaking and quacking, scratching and snapping
Howling and snorting, barking and bleating.
Don't forget the odors!
And you?
The distinguished *homo sapiens* of the lot!
Sophisticated and fragrant,
The family's pride and joy.

So,
When would you take your kids to the zoo,
To see your great-Aunt Lucy
And your third cousin Bill?
Introduce them to your kids as family.
Send them gifts;
Clothes will certainly be appreciated!
Invite them to your feasts and parties:

Not as guests that have been barbecued and boiled, fried and roasted.
How barbaric!
But family worthy of a place at the table.
Let them come without gags, shackles, or restraints.
Without besmearment, with mouthwatering sauces.....
And when will you change your family name to show your proud ancestry?
When? When?

If you care enough to let family
Sleep on bare grounds and tree branches at the zoo:
In filthy ponds and in bushes;
Eat off dirt floors and wallow in mud;
While you, family,
Sleep on mattresses in air-conditioned rooms,
Bathe in Jacuzzis and eat from Chinaware,
You really do not care.
Dare I say it is all lip service?

Imagine your great-grand kids;
Imagine, I say, your second and third cousins
Hauling **you** off to some zoo some place...
Worse, basting you in delicious marinade.
That's how **your** relatives feel right now...
Bless God; they are your relatives, not mine.

Genesis 2:7 And the LORD God formed man of the dust of the ground, and breathed into his nostrils the breath of life; and man became a living soul.

Genesis 2:19 And out of the ground the LORD God formed every beast of the field, and every fowl of the air; and brought them unto Adam to see what he would call them: and whatsoever Adam called every living creature, that was the name thereof.

Psalms 100:3 Know ye that the LORD he is God: it is he that hath made us, and not we ourselves; we are his people, and the sheep of his pasture.

Prayer

I *had* to pray yesterday,
Though they said if I did, I would pay.
I could get kicked out of school,
Then probably earn a living playing pool.
But there were some battles I had to fight,
And none of my acquaintances could ease my turmoil at night.
Peace and joy were lacking inside,
Though I looked prosperous on the outside.
I was **TIRED** of playing cool like a mannequin,
While, within me, great fires raged, as in a kiln.
Brightly colored on the exterior,
Yet lifeless and dead in the interior...
Those seeing my swagger would give me props
But they could not tell I was a walking corpse...

Then a friend (*a friend, I say!*) told me about the Lord:
The unseen One that had made me from mud.
If a pilot could entrust lives to the unseen men at the tower,
I figured I could dare trust mine with an unseen, yet higher, Power.
So I prayed Him to forgive and transform me.
Guess what, that's precisely what did He.
Now they say my face seems always aglow.
Well, that's because of the Lord I know.

Are you tired yet?

Mark 5:15 And they came to Jesus, and see him that was possessed with the devil, and had the legion, sitting, and clothed, and in his right mind: and they were afraid.

The Man

Did you just call yourself a man?
Excuse me while I laugh as hard as I can.
From their strengths, many have made fortunes for life,
While you stay home, practicing kickboxing on your wife.

"You spent your salary on gambling?" she asks,
Knowing at home there exist several unfinished tasks.
Your quick blow lays her flat on the pavement,
But how can violence be answer to an argument?

When will you come to realize
That manliness has no bearing on your fist size.
That you may be born a male,
But concerning manliness, you are quite pale.

So you want to know what a man is?
You may stop looking to your buddies.
A man leads, provides, cherishes, and preserves.
He nurtures, protects, guides, and, above all, still serves.

1 Peter 3:7 Likewise, ye husbands, dwell with them according to knowledge, giving honour unto the wife, as unto the weaker vessel, and as being heirs together of the grace of life; that your prayers be not hindered

Matthew 20:27 And whosoever will be chief among you, let him be your servant:

Matthew 23:11 But he that is greatest among you shall be your servant.

The Impressive Shell

Who are you trying to impress?
I've looked over my shoulders,
And found no one there.
[Me?]
I see your auto has a new paint job.
[So?]
I heard your stereo speakers while you were a mile away.
[I wonder how your eardrums feel?]
Those rims are spinning!
[Ahhhhh…..They cost more than the car!!!]
My goodness, your perfume could pass for bee bait.
[Your risk, not mine!]
Your appearance is really dazzling.
[Where are my sunglasses?]

So you succeeded in being a moving billboard:
Heads turning, eyes looking, ears hurting.
You have your fleeting claim to fame,
Then you go back home to mourn your emptiness.
Hollow misery.
You had hoped that all that attention
Would translate into self-worth for you.
Alas…
You will go again tomorrow,
Treading the same old mill…

I hope and pray you, one day, will realize
That fulfillment starts from within, not without.
That an impressive wrapping does not make an impressive gift:
That God has made you an impressive gift to the world, your wrapping regardless.

Psalm 39:5c ...verily every man at his best state is altogether vanity. Selah.

Matthew 23:27 Woe unto you, scribes and Pharisees, hypocrites! for ye are like unto whited sepulchres, which indeed appear beautiful outward, but are within full of dead men's bones, and of all uncleanness.

2 Corinthians 4:7 But we have this treasure in earthen vessels, that the excellency of the power may be of God, and not of us.

The Unchanger

Jesus Christ, the same
Yesterday, today, and forever.
Back then He healed the lame.
He will heal, today, anyone, whosoever.

He raised the dead and freed the prisoners,
And preached the Word to all and sundry.
He chose disciples and made them soul-winners.
He opened eyes and fed the hungry.

The crowd was set to stone the adulteress.
The Lord spoke and freed her that was captive.
Use not as an excuse to transgress,
The Lord requires us from sin to be no more active.

Give me Lord, give me Lord –
We bombard Him daily for our need,
But, for ages, He's been sowing in us, His Word.
Where is His harvest from His seed?

Yes, by His blood, He has given us victory.
Your burdens, bondages, and foes bow to His name.
But pray, how many remember the fig tree?
It wouldn't yield fruit; it had itself to blame.

Malachi 3:6 For I am the LORD, I change not; therefore ye sons of Jacob are not consumed.

Hebrews 13:8 Jesus Christ the same yesterday, and to day, and for ever.

John 15:8, 16 Herein is my Father glorified, that ye bear much fruit; so shall ye be my disciples. Ye have not chosen me, but I have chosen you, and ordained you, that ye should go and bring forth fruit, and that your fruit should remain: that whatsoever ye shall ask of the Father in my name, he may give it you.

CPSIA information can be obtained at www.ICGtesting.com
Printed in the USA
BVOW10s1427030116

431630BV00010B/39/P

9 781498 442299